## ABOUT GARLIC

Gives the historical background to this amazing herb and shows how its miraculous healing powers can protect your health and assist the cure of many and varied complaints. Gives hints on its use in the kitchen and includes recipes for garlic flavoured dishes.

D1545991

# ABOUT GARLIC

### The Supreme Herbal Remedy

*by*
G. J. BINDING
M.B.E., F.R.H.S.

THORSONS PUBLISHERS LIMITED
Wellingborough, Northamptonshire

First published 1970
Eighth Impression 1980

ISBN 0 7225 0148 X

Printed in Great Britain by
Hunt Barnard Printing Ltd., Aylesbury, Bucks.

# CONTENTS

## REFERENCES

*British Medical Journal:* 10/8/68 and 29/3/69.

*New York Times:* 4/3/69.

*Herbal Simples* by W. T. Fernie, M.D. (1895—reprinted 1914).

*Nature's Medicines—The Folklore, Romance and Value of Herbal Medicines* by R. Lucas.

*My Experiences with Living Food* by Kristine Nolfi, M.D.

*The Home Book of Health* by D. Gunn, M.D. (1878).

GARLIC IS A HERB which nowadays the average English family does not make much use of, or accept, either as a food, or for its medicinal powers. This has not always been the case, for until about 100 years ago this little herb played a prominent part in our kitchens, and was widely used by doctors and herbalists alike. Members of the medical profession and nature cure Practitioners, one and all, proclaimed garlic to have miraculous healing powers. Together with many other fine herbs, such as parsley, it could be seen growing in gardens everywhere. Alas, except for parsley few have really survived to be cultivated on a large scale today by the average English gardener or allotment holder. The reasons for the decline in use of garlic are varied. Many refrain from even trying this herb because it has such an extra strong pungent smell. The ever expanding world wide marketing and constant discovery of new drugs has caused the medical profession, and others, to turn away from and neglect herbal medicine and natural healing. Garlic can only be cultivated on a large commercial scale in warmer climates with long summers. This fact deters farmers or market gardeners in England from growing a crop not in such great demand and likely to receive a setback from our unpredictable weather. It can also be imported very cheaply at perhaps even less than it would cost to grow over here. Some may think that garlic is a food produced mainly in warmer countries and fit only for the inhabitants of such lands. This herb can, of course, be cultivated in the south and south western part of England with fairly good results if planted early on a sunny site and allowed a long growing period. The writer has grown it for many years, mainly as a matter of interest in the cultivation of the more unusual type of vegetables. Bulbs of garlic can be purchased from many greengrocers shops throughout the year for a few pence, so in this respect it is not worth the time and trouble involved in planting it, when the crop is grown in such abundance in Mediterranean countries, and sold so cheaply in England.

It is hoped that this little booklet about an amazing herb will give some idea of the role garlic has played throughout history as a food and medicine. It will be shown how it can protect our health and assist the cure of many and varied complaints. Evidence of its wonderful healing powers going back to a time before recorded history will be given, so readers will be able to judge for themselves what a remarkable little herb it really is, and has been from time immemorial.

More and more people today, becoming disturbed by the increasing administration of drugs for all and every illness, are looking again to old fashioned herbal remedies. There are signs that many herbs, including garlic, are once again being more widely accepted. It is being shipped from such far-away countries as South Africa and is displayed more frequently on shelves with other more accepted vegetables. Health food manufacturers are able to produce garlic capsules and tablets which are odourless. This is made possible by the combination of other herbs with the garlic, such as parsley and because the capsule does not have to be chewed in the mouth. In spite of this there are still many who are most vague about garlic and what it can do for us.

In the last chapter ways of becoming gradually acquainted with this potent herb are shown, together with its use in soups, salads, main courses and cooking in general.

This brief account of the historical background and use of garlic as a food and medicine, may answer some if not all of your queries.

# CHAPTER ONE

# THE ONION FAMILY

I**T** I**S** N**OT** generally realized that there are at least 15 different species of onions grown throughout the world. During the past 16 years the writer has been fortunate to be able to cultivate and sample most of them. The ordinary onion for everyday use in the kitchen again may be subdivided into numerous strains produced to suit all tastes and needs.

*Cultivation*

Onions like a rich medium-to-light soil although not freshly manured. They will only thrive and really do well on a good sunny location. The finest specimens and largest onions are produced in such countries as Spain, where long hours of sunshine makes for massive growth. Even today Spanish onion sellers can sometimes still be seen in England, their cycles loaded with giant onions. Successful onion growing in England is really an art which can only be acquired by practice and attention to detail. Like runner beans and a few other vegetables, onions may be grown on the same site for years. Therefore, it is really worth getting a soil really suited to this fine crop. A good farmyard (stable) manure or vegetable compost should have been dug in the previous autumn.

Although this book deals with garlic we must take a brief look at the entire onion family, as some species are more closely related to garlic than others. All onions have been widely proclaimed and accepted as excellent food value for centuries.

*Onion Sets*

Much of the trial and error and other problems concerning the cultivation of onions have been overcome by the production of many types of onion sets. Before 1939 these sets were imported from America and other countries. They proved valuable to gardeners who had difficulty in growing onions from seed. Such sets are nowadays grown on a large scale in the south of England. These sets are little onions in a very early stage of growth. When replanted in the spring they continue to grow to full size onions. They are practically immune from disease and seldom bolt. *Stuttgarter Giant* is a very fine species of onion obtained in sets which really do grow to an enormous size. Unlike the globular shaped onion they have a flat bottom. There are many more strains of household onion which can be grown from either seeds or sets.

### Spring Onion

Grown quickly in spring and served with salad, sold by all greengrocers.

### Welsh Onion

A native of Siberia and not so well known in England. Its name is said to have come from the German word *Walseh* (meaning foreign) or because long ago this onion was accepted and much liked by the people of Wales. Each plant produces bunches of long bulblets which are dug up and served like spring onions. The foliage can be used in salads throughout the year. Reputed to be an everlasting species—but for best results should be renewed every few years by splitting up existing plants.

### Tree or Egyptian Onion

Came from Canada and seldom grown in England. This is unfortunate for it is a tough plant which will survive the most severe winters. It will thrive under more exacting conditions that other onions. Ideal for salads and cocktails, it bears bunches of small onions at the top of stems—hence the name tree onion.

## Potato Onion

This variety forms clusters of bulbs about the size of shallots on or just below the surface of the soil. It can be grown quickly and has a mild flavour.

## Japanese Bunching Onions

Sown as seeds, these plants are not fully grown till the second year. They resemble large chives and are without bulbs. A great advantage is that unlike chives the green shoots are available throughout the winter. There are two edible parts. Shoots used as chives and the silvery white stems resembling small leeks and known as scallions may be served as a salad onion.

## Evergreen Bunching Onions

A useful perennial onion mainly grown in the U.S.A. It produces scallions which are used the same as Japanese onions. Very resistant to frost and up to six shoots grow the first year from one onion.

## Chives

The smallest and finest flavoured of the entire onion family. Both bulbs and leaves can be consumed. An ideal onion for persons unable to eat stronger varieties. Will thrive in indifferent soils.

## Leek

A very ancient English vegetable still growing wild in many parts. In Egypt the cultivation of the leek goes back to the days of the Bible. It became the National Emblem of Wales in the 6th century.

*Saffron*

Rarely grown nowadays. In older times the stigmas were dried and used as a flavouring and for colouring cheese butter cakes.

*Liquorice*

Used as flavour for confectionery, drinks, and years ago for making chewing tobacco.

*Reflexed Leaved Sedum*

Very uncommon today. Formerly utilized as a salad onion and for adding flavour to soups.

*Rocambole or Sand Leek*

Again a vegetable unfortunately seldom cultivated today. It is very similar to Garlic.

*Shallots*

This vegetable was first brought to England by the Crusaders returning from Syria in the Middle Ages, and has flourished ever since. It came from the town of Ascalon from which the present-day name shallot is derived. Like nearly all the other onion family it needs a soil in good heart, having been manured the previous year. It grows rapidly and is extensively cultivated by gardeners and allotment holders. Its growing habit is similar to garlic, with which it has much in common, being almost as equally pungent in smell. Unlike garlic, a large number of green shoots are produced from each shallot. It always seems a shame that these shoots are mostly left to grow yellow and die off as the shallots mature. Gather one or two at a time from each plant: on being cut up into small pieces they make a wonderful addition to a salad. A fine health giving green vegetable rich in vitamin C, provided soon after winter, when other vegetables are in short supply. Nearly all growers use their crops of shallots for pickling. If on sale in shops they are likewise displayed as onions for pickling. Shallots consumed raw, with wholemeal bread and cheese, make a feast fit for a king. They have to be tried to be appreciated, but once eaten can be enjoyed always; you will never want to pickle them again. A fine vegetable like the shallot, with all the characteristics of garlic, deserves a place on the table, not to be allowed to lie for months on end in a jar of vinegar.

## Garlic

A perennial herb of the lily family, garlic grows into bulbs comprising up to 20 or more cloves. There are three kinds, the most popular being the common white variety, so called owing to the silvery white skin covering bulbs and cloves. There is pink garlic which grows earlier than the white, and a red coloured bulb, a slower grower that produces much larger cloves.

## Cultivation

Garlic needs a light sandy soil, plenty of sun, with a long growing season to produce large bulbs and cloves. A site which has been previously manured for another crop is ideal. No fresh manure other than bone meal should be added. In the warmer south west, plantings may be carried out in November: for other parts of the south, February is quite soon enough. Select cloves only from the outside of the bulbs and cover with half an inch of soil. Eight inches should be allowed between each plant and one foot separating rows. Apart from weeding and using the hoe, no other attention is necessary. Differing from shallots, cloves of garlic produce only one large stem. As these leaves turn yellow during July and August they are allowed to die off. Bulbs can then be harvested and allowed to dry thoroughly in the sun. After being tied in bunches they can be hung in a dry frost free place till required for use.

## Wild Garlic

A herb found in damp lands in Western countries. This species of garlic was later taken to the U.S.A. This herb was also known as *Sauce Alone*, *Jack-by-the-Hedge* or *Hedge Garlic*. Of the mustard family, it grows to a height of about three feet and has a tap root. It was at one time one of the most frequently grown potherbs of the old English cottage gardens. Mostly known as *Sauce Alone*, it would thrive equally among hedgerows, in woods and even on waste ground.

Having taken a brief look at all members of this quite extensive onion family, we find that the nearest relation to garlic is the humble shallot, but more especially the *Rocambole* or *Sand Leek*. So before leaving the family, a few more details about this most unusual and rarely grown vegetable are given.

## Giant Garlic

A certain amount of confusion may exist because many species of onions and garlic are given different names. This is so with *Giant Garlic*, which is really another name for the *Rocambole* or *Sand Leek*. Many of these vegetables with a difference came to England from countries overseas. This often accounts for a herb or vegetable being known by two or more names. This applies to *Giant Garlic* or *Rocambole*, which is really a native of Denmark. A great attraction about this vegetable is that, although to all intents and purposes it is in fact garlic, it has a much milder flavour. *Rocambole* should appeal to persons to whom garlic may prove too strong, or for others who would prefer a less pungent herb.

Although gardeners in general may not bother to grow their own garlic when a bulb can be purchased for a few coppers, greater interest and attraction lies in cultivating the sister variety *Rocambole*. This kind can seldom, if ever, be purchased in England. Growing conditions similar for garlic—on a sunny location. Being somewhat like the Egyptian onion in growth, it will reach a height of about 3 feet. Long slender stems are produced, which require staking if the land is exposed. New bulbs of garlic will appear and grow on the top of the stems. These bulbs are only about one eighth of an inch thick, being closely interlaced. The plant gives off a strong garlic smell. Cloves may be used in the same manner as garlic. In Denmark it is very much prized for flavouring cheeses.

### Garlic Pear

A tree from Jamaica which bears a fruit having a strong smell of garlic.

### Garlic Shrubs

There are a number of these whose foliage, when bruised, has the strong odour of garlic.

### Ramson or Wild Garlic

This was so named after the ram owing to its strong lingering smell.

# CHAPTER TWO

# HISTORY OF GARLIC IN ENGLAND

To SEPARATE MYTHOLOGY, folklore and old wives' tales, which have been woven around this little herb for centuries, we must look back in history a long way. Cultivation of garlic took place long before records were kept. The country of its origin is therefore not very clear but believed to be southern Europe, where it is still grown on a large scale and made part of the diet of the peoples of such countries. Garlic was one of the numerous herbs grown and used extensively in England until about 100 years ago. Together with onions and shallots it shares a record of being one of the oldest vegetables cultivated by man. What is the truth about this herb with such a vast reputation and said to have almost miraculous healing powers?

This herb, a perennial vegetable of the Lily family, is not only used as a food and medicine but has a long historical background. Although a permanent plant, best results for cultivation are achieved by splitting up cloves from bulbs and replanting annually. For best results only the outside cloves of reasonable size are used. Garlic, owing to its very pungent smell, needs no introduction anywhere, even to those who have never sampled or even seen it. The peculiar unmistakable penetrating odour of this herb is caused by its main ingredient, which is a volatile oil. This is very unfortunate, for many more people would be tempted to try garlic except for this strong, lingering smell. However, if the odour is removed with it will go most, if not all of the powerful healing properties of this herb, as this booklet will show.

*Varieties of Garlic*

There are several species of this herb but only about four are mainly used in Europe. These include white garlic, the most common kind, with a silvery white skin which is displayed by many greengrocers and delicatessen shops. There are pink bulbs, which grow quicker and also a red type which is slower to mature and produces fewer but much larger cloves per bulb than the white and pink varieties. Finally, we have *Giant Garlic* or *Rocambole* sometimes called *Sand Leek. Rocambole*, a native of Denmark, is a very much neglected species of the garlic family, which has the attraction of being far less potent than the others.

*Garlic in England*

This ancient herb is believed to have been brought to Britain by the Romans during their occupation. It was used with great success and prized by old time herbalists, long before the discovery of drugs. (A later chapter deals with garlic and Herbal Medicine.) Until about 100 years ago this herb was extensively used by family doctors.

*The Great Plague*

So much may be said for and against the use of this noxious herb, which was at one time called stinkweed. It is interesting to note that in 1665, whilst the Great Plague ravished the land, and people were dying in thousands from this terrible pestilence, the entire occupants of one house in Chester survived. The reason given was that the cellars of this dwelling contained a large supply of garlic, which kept the occupants free from the effects of the dreaded plague. This was recorded in history and the particular house was subsequently named 'God's Provident House'. This well-known Tudor house still exists today and it is open to the public.

## Other Plagues of the Middle Ages

Throughout Europe during the visitation of so many horrible plagues it became common knowledge that those who had made garlic part of their diet survived. This herb was also used to disinfect burial grounds, thereby helping to keep the pestilence from spreading.

## World Wars

During the terrible carnage of the War of 1914/18, garlic was used with great success for treating the wounded in battle areas. The amazing antiseptic power of this herb not only saved thousands of lives but prevented such complications and serious infections as gangrene. During this long struggle garlic played a vital role in checking the spread of such ghastly epidemics as typhus and dysentery. It proved a godsend and countless more lives would have been lost without it. In World War II garlic again proved invaluable for treating wounded soldiers and the Medical Services used thousands of tons of this herb. Great credit must be given to this little member of the onion family, for during the 1939/45 war there was not one case of septic poisoning or gangrene among wounded servicemen fortunate enough to receive timely treatment. This record alone should put garlic high on the list of antiseptics for ever.

## Drugs Gradually Replace Herbs

Since the unfortunate decline in the use of herbs, the demand for garlic in England has naturally not been so great. However, since the last war when thousands visited the continent and Mediterranean countries, a greater interest has followed in the way of life of these lands, including food preparation and the use of garlic. Many more families nowadays are able to spend holidays abroad; this too has stimulated an interest in the dishes of the continent and southern European countries. However, even today the vast majority of people in this country would endorse the ruling of the ancient Greeks, which banned those who had been eating garlic from the temple of the Goddess Cybele. Although practically everywhere drugs have replaced herbs, there are indications that herbal medicine is slowly but surely being revived.

### Future of Garlic in England

Does garlic have a role to play both as a food and medicine, for use by doctors and in hospitals in the variety of ways in which it can be employed? The answer to this question would most definitely appear to be 'Yes'. There are growing signs that more people are becoming accustomed to garlic in spite of it being hot and possessing such an overpowering odour. Greengrocers invariably stock supplies and it is being more widely accepted as part of the diet, or used as a medicine. Many immigrants in England today are from warm or semi-tropical lands and are used to eating this herb and continue to do so.

Many people are not happy or prepared to put up with the 'hit or miss' system of the National Health Service. More are taking a greater interest in their own health and desire some form of preventative medical treatment. On the continent, especially in Germany, the signs are even more promising—they have thousands of our equivalent of the Health Food Stores—known by the Germans as the *Reform Haus*—and what a wonderful reformation these shops have to offer. We have to thank a German doctor named Hofels for being the first person to produce garlic in capsule form.

### Health Food Stores

An increasing number of Health Food Stores are being opened today and there are at present over 600 throughout the country. A number of old established companies produce large amounts of herbal and vitamin supplements, including garlic, in a variety of forms. By various means this herb may be rendered tasteless and odourless but can still retain its amazing properties for healing. When the oil is produced in tablet form parsley is sometimes added, which is rich in vitamin C and serves the useful purpose of counteracting the smell of the garlic. If raw garlic has been eaten, the resultant smell can be partially removed if parsley is chewed afterwards.

## Introduction of Garlic Pearles

In 1920 a Mr. J. A. Hofels, who was a doctor in Germany, came to live in England. Having made an extensive study of garlic in the usual methodical German manner, and knowing from his experience as a medical man what a wonderful food and medicine it was, Herr Hofels discovered ways and means of encapsulating the oil from the garlic. He decided it was vital to overcome peoples' prejudice against this herb because of its pungent smell and hot taste. From specially grown crops he produced garlic pearles, which have proved a tremendous success and are used in many countries throughout the world. This in fact made a revolution in the taking of this herb as a supplementary food or medicine. All the essential vital oils of the herb have been retained in capsule form. What is also important is that it can be taken without tainting the breath as digestion does not start until after the pearle has been swallowed. This is not the case when raw garlic is eaten, for then the smell is mostly projected from the back of the throat.

## Wonderful Aid for the Lungs

Bronchitis being very widespread in England, it is often referred to on the continent as being 'The English Disease'. How miraculous this little herb is for improving and safeguarding the entire breathing tract! Many unfortunate sufferers from chronic bronchitis gradually get emphysema through living in cold, damp, and sometimes foggy winters. Garlic would undoubtedly work wonders for such persons, and give them a new lease of life, as our little booklet will show.

# CHAPTER THREE

# GARLIC IN ANCIENT CIVILIZATIONS

APART FROM EGYPT many other civilizations existing long before the Christian era are shown to have accepted garlic as a food and medicine. Like the Egyptians they also greatly valued the miraculous healing powers and preventive treatment of this herb for practically every illness then known. It is still as widely used as ever in many of these lands. From the introduction and cultivation of garlic in England we now go back to times long before the birth of Christ.

### Babylonians

Over 3000 B.C. in the Eastern Mediterranean the people of Babylon used garlic, which they considered miraculous. In those remote times the herb was accepted as a food and powerful medicine. Some complaints treated by garlic included all respiratory infections and illnesses of the breathing tract, skin complaints, leprosy, to prevent plagues and epidemics, against worms and a host of other germ destroying uses.

### Ancient Greece

Another great race which has left its impact on civilization today, the Ancient Greeks, accepted and used garlic extensively before the days of the Bible. This great race of people became garlic lovers, for they found the herb invaluable for treating every malady and as part of their diet. Famous Greek Philosopher Aristotle (384 B.C.) had this to say about the pungent herb, "It is a cure for hydrophobia and a tonic, is hot, laxative, but bad for the eyes". Hippocrates (460 B.C.) also praised the merits of garlic which he considered as a sudorific (medicine that promotes perspiration) and good as both a laxative and diuretic (medicine to aid secretion of urine). Aristophanes (444 B.C.), a famous Greek comedian and author, thought so highly of garlic, that he said the juice would restore virility in men. He also wrote of those famous Greek athletes eating the herb to put them on their mettle for exercises at the stadium. The performance and wonderful physiques of these ancient Greek athletes were a great credit to them, and would be for any nation in the 20th century.


*The Most Famous Greek Philosopher*

Together with Plato, who was his tutor, Aristotle was undoubtedly one of the most famous of all Greeks. He was so well thought of that he became personal tutor to Alexander the Great. Aristotle was a most meticulous investigator and until the advent of modern science was regarded as a foremost authority on physics and biology. To refer back to his comments on garlic outlined in the previous paragraph when he said, "It is a cure for Hydrophobia and a tonic", we may be certain his very favourable comments on this herb were given only after prolonged study and experience. You may be sure that these were true facts in ancient Greece, and are equally so today, as it is hoped this booklet will convince you from the evidence given. It may be of interest that Aristotle was considered a world expert on biology, which concerns, "That science of life, that branch of knowledge which treats of organized beings or animals and plants". This definition of biology adds strength to the belief that the wise man's comments on garlic were well founded.

## Olympic Games

Aristophanes wrote over 400 years before Christ of those Greek athletes eating garlic to improve their performance at the stadium. Little did this author realize all those centuries ago that the Olympic Games would become so famous. For nearly 12 centuries the games were held from 776 B.C. to A.D. 394. They were revived in 1896 and except for the war years have been held ever since. Garlic gave those ancient Greeks strength and stamina for the games as it will for others today.

## The Roman Empire

One of the most dominant races of the old world, the Romans, conquered and occupied practically every country. A famous Roman author and poet named Virgil (70-19 B.C.) was an expert on, and wrote much about, the arts of husbandry and care of cattle and bees. This learned man had this to say about garlic, "That it was essential to maintain the strength of the harvesters".

Galen (A.D. 131-200) was a most famous Roman physician and lecturer whose methods of teaching dominated medicine for over 1,000 years. He practised and taught medicine in Rome and was acknowledged far and wide, by all, including the Emperor Marcus Aurelius, as their greatest physician. Galen spoke highly about garlic, which he called *Theriaca Rusticoriam*. Translated into English, it means "Poor Man's Treacle". What a fine, health giving treacle it has proved to be! Galen also maintained that this herb was the finest antidote against poison. (In the light of modern knowledge it would now be more accurate to say that garlic helps to eradicate toxins in the blood stream.) So the leading doctor of the mighty Roman Empire could not speak too highly of this food and medicine, of the humble little garlic herb.

## The Roman Army

A Greek doctor named Discorides was chief physician to the Roman Army in the 2nd century A.D. He prescribed garlic for all lung complaints, stomach and intestinal disorders among troops. He also used it as a most effective vermifuge (expellor of intestinal worms). Roman soldiers ate garlic in the belief that it made them brave and courageous in battle. The fact that this army conquered the then known world speaks well of their fitness and for the herb.

## Celsus

During the 1st century A.D. Celsus became a famous Roman author. One of his classical works was a massive Encyclopedia dealing with farming, medicine, military art and many other subjects. The medical knowledge contained in this work became a basic source for the History of Alexandrian Medicine, which became a masterpiece surpassed only by the works of Hippocrates and Galen. Celsus held a moderate attitude between empiricism and methodism, theory and practice were equally indispensable to him. Celsus claimed that garlic was a cure for many illnesses, including fevers and all intestinal disorders.

Credit goes, rightly so, to the ancient Greeks and Romans for laying the foundation stones of Western Civilization, though naturally the teachings of Jesus have played a most vital part. However, the methodical organized way of life and government built up by the Romans and Greeks allowed Christianity to develop and become a world wide religion.

## Phoenicians and Vikings

The Phoenicians, a very ancient but remarkable race of people, lived along a narrow strip of land between the Eastern end of the Mediterranean and mountains west of the River Jordan. It was very fertile land and they were able to cultivate an abundance of every kind of fruit and vegetables, including garlic. They grew rich by trading and became famous as seamen and miners. Expert shipbuilders, they learnt navigation from the stars, becoming carriers of the world's goods. They explored every sea and sailed to all known parts of the world, reaching Italy, Spain, France and England. These skilful mariners were ardent believers in a diet which included garlic. On their long adventurous sea voyages they always took a good supply of this herb. The fact that they endured such hardships and sailed so far in primitive vessels, across unknown seas, shows how courageous and fit they were.

### Hebrews

In prehistoric times in the country that became The Holy Land, Palestine, and is now the new State of Israel, garlic has always played an important role. The dwellers of this historic land endorsed the findings of all the other great empires on how miraculous the aromatic little herb is as both a food and medicine. Even today, in an age of modern drugs, garlic plays a vital role in Israel, it is still part of the Hebrew Talmudic rule which decrees that it be used in certain dishes and on special occasions. The Israelis still cultivate large crops of garlic for such a small country: much of it is exported.

### Bulgaria

A country where garlic has been made part of the diet for centuries. In Bulgaria today a remarkable number of people live to a very great age. They all practically without exception make garlic part of their daily food. Ordinary people have cultivated the habit of chewing this herb in much the same way as tobacco was at one time used for chewing. The great record of longevity shows that the Bulgarians are a very robust race of people. Many of them still carry out a full day's work at 100 years of age or older. The little herb undoubtedly plays a part in the remarkable achievements of this healthy nation.

*Medical Literature*

Throughout Medical History mention is made of this herb in the ancient writings and scrolls of these great empires.

# CHAPTER FOUR

## ANCIENT EGYPT

WITHOUT DOUBT THE greatest man who ever lived, to the Egyptians and many other Middle and Far Eastern Races, was Mohammed, The Prophet. There are millions of Mohammedans, followers of his faith, throughout the world. This is what he said about garlic, "In cases of stings and bites by poisonous animals, garlic acts as a theriac. Applied to the spot bitten by viper, or sting of a scorpion, it produces successful results". Knowing from personal experience how Egypt and other Middle Eastern countries abound in crawly things (every other stone you turn over in some parts of Egypt reveals a scorpion), it's a godsend that such a wonderful herbal remedy as garlic has always been grown there.

### The Pyramids

No doubt the most famous features about Egypt are the renowned Pyramids and Sphinx, being classed as one of the seven wonders of the world. Not so many people may be aware of the fact that the Egyptians cultivate and consume large amounts of garlic, leeks, onions and shallots and have done so for centuries. Garlic has a long history in the Middle East and is prominent in the *Materia Medica* of the ancient Egyptians and Hebrews. Shallots were first found being cultivated in the nearby country of Syria. Is there any connection between the colossal building project of the Pyramids and the even more ancient little garlic herb ? In the Holy Bible, Herodotus (11. 125) tells of an inscription on the Great Pyramid Cheops which listed garlic as one of the vegetables supplied in large quantities to the workers, and he also said they had lots of radishes. Ancient history shows that the first strike ever known occurred during the building of these massive tombs. It was by the thousands of Egyptian slaves constructing the pyramid Cheops. They downed tools, not over a tea break, but because their daily supply of garlic had been withheld. This herb they felt was vital and necessary for strength, stamina and endurance to carry out their gigantic task. So nearly 5,000 years ago, without garlic, they felt incapable of building the Pyramids. There is then some relationship between garlic and this inspiring building project, even if it can only be attributed to bringing about the first industrial dispute on record. Had these ancient Egyptians been permanently deprived of their smelly herb, perhaps the pyramids would not be with us to ponder over in the 20th century. Even today building and engineering experts are still baffled as to the means employed in constructing these remarkable tombs, which they consider are almost a miracle. So take advice from these ancient Egyptians and let garlic work wonders for you, not in constructing massive tombs, but in helping to build a strong healthy body, free from so many complaints prevalent in our society today.

## Onions Galore

The Egyptians past and present have not only cultivated garlic on a large scale but have always grown masses of onions, shallots and leeks. One particular species of onion has always been known as the *Egyptian onion*.

In some respects onions and garlic are identical, but the Egyptians considered garlic to be something much more than just another onion. It became their mainstay as a food and a cure for nearly all illnesses. Their medicine chests of cloves of garlic provided treatment for cures for such complaints as:

all intestinal disorders; skin infections and diseases; worms; flatulence; every infection of the respiratory tract and for treating the wounded in battle. Most important, above all they considered that this little herb with the mighty reputation would counteract the symptoms of ageing. One may well say, all these wonderful claims for garlic are very fine and may have worked miracles for the Egyptians but what about us? In this respect it is interesting to note that the dwellers of the Nile Delta were not alone in their praise of garlic. As outlined in the previous paragraph, many other mighty empires endorsed the belief that garlic was a miracle food and health restorer and would cure or prevent all the complaints mentioned in the *Materia Medica* of Ancient Egypt.

### Egypt in the 20th Century

In the years before the 2nd World War there were some 3,000,000 fellahin (peasants or agricultural labourers) in the Nile Delta existing on less than a shilling a day. Indeed, a poverty-stricken nation, even by pre-war standards, yet in spite of this Egypt ranked high for a small nation in world sporting events which demanded great strength and endurance. They were able to produce some of the strongest men to take part in the sport of weight lifting and many Egyptians gained high awards.

### Channel Swimmers

Up till 1965 Egyptian swimmers have succeeded in swimming the Channel on nine occasions. Only six men in the world have swum the Channel both ways, and two of them were Egyptian. For such a small, poor nation to produce even a handful of world champions shows that the endurance and stamina of those remarkable builders of the pyramids still exists today.

## A Land of Garlic

As a young apprentice on board ships of The Prince Line in the early 1930's the writer made trips into the Mediterranean. Life in the ancient seaport of Alexandria was always very fascinating with 14 miles of seafront and beautiful beaches. As soon as a ship docked, swarms of excited Arab stevedores would be all over the vessel. Trinket and souvenir sellers and other less desirable characters would also make their appearance. It was in this colourful port that I first became acquainted with that aromatic little garlic herb. During our stay in dock the job of watching cargo was carried out. This entailed checking every item of goods loaded on or off the ship and brought close contact with the agents, Arab foremen and others in authority. One could never forget the impressive dress of many of these persons, their smiling faces showing mouths filled with masses of gold teeth, and, as a finishing touch, the never-ending fumes of garlic. They are a very voluble and excitable race of people and spend hours shouting, jostling and cursing each other, Arabic being the ideal language for this. Never at any time did they attempt to hide the fact that garlic was part of their diet. This was my first introduction to garlic, with its pungent smell, in the noisy atmosphere of a ship working cargo, in the blazing Egyptian sun.

For many years the open display by these Arabs of their love and daily use of garlic caused me to regard it as being most undesirable to partake of in any shape or form.

## Becoming a Convert

Later years spent in Egypt, the Sudan, Palestine and the Far East gradually caused me to take a greater interest in the foods of these countries. Slowly, over long years, I came to regard garlic in a far more kindly light, especially when the historical background of this herb became known to me and I realized what it could do for people, even in this modern age. Like those Arabs of so long ago, the writer must confess he too became a lover of garlic, and has been one ever since.

This herb has for generations proved to be a wonderful aid in keeping healthy, and I feel it should, in moderation, be made part of the diet of everyone who is able to consume it without ill effects. Naturally it is a very strong smelling food; were it not so the healing powers would be ineffective, as this book will show. Many are prejudiced against garlic because of its odour; this must be overcome and the herb given a try. For those persons unable to accept such a strong food there are many excellent garlic tablets, capsules or pearles readily available from Health Food shops. These can be swallowed and are odourless. Others are not prepared to consume a food which is Eastern in origin. Once these two problems have been overcome and garlic is sampled in some of its many forms, you, like myself and the Arabs, will become a lover of it for the rest of your life. Apart from all its wonderful attributes from a health point of view, the fact is that it adds so much to a simple meal. It seems that nature made this little herb so tasty and satisfying that once a person gets used to it he or she becomes an addict. Everybody should want to become fond of such a health giving food. To an everyday meal such as a cottage pie, it will add so much as to turn it into a feast, every morsel of which will be thoroughly enjoyed. So besides making an ordinary meal fit for a banquet it will bring health-giving properties seldom, if ever, found in any single herb. Being superior to every other member of the onion family, it stands out on its own, a very fine though often neglected herb. Try it and see for yourself.

# CHAPTER FIVE

# FRANCE

LIKE MANY OTHER southern European countries with long sunny summers, France has always been able to cultivate such crops as garlic. This herb has been used all over France for a long time in cookery and as a medicine.

During the year 1100 A.D. Robert of Normandy had this to say about garlic, "Sith garlic then hath poure to save from death. Bear with it though it make unsavoure breathe".

## *Plague in Marseilles*

Have you ever sampled a vinegar in France known as "Four Thieves Vinegar"? Do you know how this unusual name came about? Marseilles, the bustling seaport in southern France, suffered a terrible plague in 1721. Records show that it took a very heavy toll and was more devastating than the Great Plague of London. Thousands of people were dying like flies and it was becoming increasingly difficult to find anyone to bury the corpses. Government officials decided to release four convicts from prison who were under sentence of death for theft and make them perform this last service for some of the unfortunate victims. A remarkable thing was these thieves seemed to be completely immune from the plague in spite of being exposed continuously in carrying out their gruesome task. Nobody could understand how these men had escaped the horror of the plague. After it was over they were offered their freedom if they shared the secret of how they managed to avoid contacting the dreaded pestilence. It was then revealed that each day they drank wine with a macerate of garlic. This concoction immediately became famous as "*Vinaigre des Quatre Voleurs*" (Four Thieves Vinegar), which it is still called today. Another version of this story is that the convicts confessed to stealing from bodies whilst being safeguarded against the plague by their potent drink. One of these stories may be true but the fact remains that The Four Thieves Vinegar became famous and is still with us today to add some credence to the narrative. In turn others believe that a certain Richard Forhave produced and sold this drink. It became known as Forhaves but as time went by the name became misinterpreted as "Four Thieves". So you may take your pick of the manner in which this drink came into being.

### Poor Man's Treacle

Also in France this herb is sometimes called "*Theriaque Des Pauvres*", which is translated as Poor Man's Treacle. The meaning is that the person may be poor financially but will reap wonderful health-giving benefits from his treacle.

### French Authors

Franklin wrote in *Lavie d'autrefois* that during the 16th century the people of Paris consumed garlic with butter during spring. They were firmly convinced that this habit improved their health for the entire year. People in provinces of France take a diet of this herb for 2-3 weeks upon the first fresh butter of spring. Also during the 16th century it was revealed that many doctors in France carried cloves of garlic to safeguard themselves and their patients from epidemic diseases. This fact was made known by a Dr. Felix Bremond in his writing, *Dictionaire de la Table*.

A soup consisting of garlic and onions is considered very effective in curing a hangover, so much so that it is called *Soupe à Lyvriogne*.

*Legends, Folklore and Mythology*

Mythology is the study of stories about gods and immortals, monsters and heroes. For centuries garlic has had a tremendous prestige for its ability to repel evil. It was therefore considered to act like magic against darkness, and all the terrible forebodings that might take place after sunset.

Garlic was sometimes called "stinkweed". A very old Mohammedan legend is that, "When Satan walked from the garden of Eden, garlic appeared from the ground where his left foot rested and an onion sprouted at his right foot". Pliny the Naturalist considered a magnet would become powerless if brought into close contact with the herb. The Ancient Greeks were in the habit of putting bulbs of garlic on piles of stones at cross roads. This, it was said, provided a supper for Hecate, the underworld goddess of charms and enchantment. Yet another story is that garlic was given to Odysseus to overcome the effects of the potions of Circe. Bullfighters are known to carry pieces of this pungent herb, which it is said will prevent the bulls from charging.

In some countries, even in the 20th century, in India in particular, garlic is worn for protection against witches, demons, vampires and the Evil Eye. Bulbs would be hung over doors especially to dispel evil after darkness. Perhaps they consider the strong smell of this herb is sufficient to scare anything away.

# CHAPTER SIX

# THE TRUTH ABOUT GARLIC

WE HAVE FOLLOWED the path of this ancient herb throughout history, from the time when the first cloves were being planted in the rich soils of those warm Mediterranean climates of southern Europe till the 20th century. The views of authors, herbalists and comments of famous leaders, doctors and others have been recorded. What then are the true facts about garlic? For the answer to this question we must look to the scientists and nutrition experts of more recent times.

## Fernie's Herbal Simples

There follows an extract from a famous book written by a Doctor W. Fernie, M.D., in 1897. In his *Herbal Simples* he has this to say about garlic. "The bulb consisting of several combined cloves, is stimulating, antispasmodic, expectorant and diuretic. Its active properties depend on an essential oil which may readily be obtained by distillation. A medicinal tincture is made with spirit of wine, of which from 10 to 20 drops may be taken in water several times a day. Garlic proves useful in asthma, whooping cough and other spasmodic affections of the chest. For an adult one or two cloves may be eaten at a time." How much truth is there in these writings of Dr. Fernie from over 80 years ago? Let us see how modern experts not only endorse his views but give proof.

## Garlic and the Scientist

A world-wide research into the so-called miracles of

garlic has been taking place for a number of years. Slowly but surely dedicated men in laboratories in many countries have proved scientifically, beyond dispute, what those learned men and herbalists had to find out for themselves by trial and error methods centuries ago. These experiments have taken place in such varied places as Japan, America, France and Germany. They have conclusively shown that garlic will do the following things for us. Reduce blood pressure. That is it good as an anthelmintic (worm destroyer) and will produce good results against intestinal putrefaction. Also it has wonderful antiseptic properties and all kinds of bacteria will be killed by chopped up pieces of garlic in minutes. In the U.S.S.R. garlic is known as Russian penicillin because of its amazing results in treating the wounded in two world wars. By placing the herb around the infected wounds, within a few days they were clean. The Russians suffered more casualties than all the other allied nations together. They have introduced methods of inhaling garlic after reducing it to a vapour.

## America

In the U.S.A. as in England, for many years garlic has not really been accepted. However, since the end of the last war the Americans have made rapid developments in both experiments with and the use of this herb. They endorse the belief known centuries ago that garlic is ideal for use in all respiratory infections, bronchitis and asthma. Also it will aid the development of healthy bacteria in the intestines. In all cases they found garlic to be harmless with no side or after-effects. It was also shown to be a wonderful preventative against tuberculosis, pneumonia, diphtheria and typhus. Being a great aid to the digestion, it can kill all manner of worms and is a food for the nerves. America is one of the world's largest growers of garlic. The State of California cultivates more than any other State in the U.S.A. In 1960 the total cash crop of garlic in U.S.A. equalled $1,800,000.

## Vitamin and Mineral Content

Whatever may be said in support or against the use of garlic as a food and medicine one cannot get away from the evidence of the composition of this herb. It contains a certain amount of protein and calcium, is rich in potassium and phosphorus and has a supply of vitamins B and C. Taking all this goodness into consideration, we are certainly getting good value for money in the purchase of a bulb of garlic for a few pence. Even if we only believe a fraction of what herbalists and public figures have said for generations, we cannot dispute scientific evidence.

It is appreciated that the vitamin and mineral content of this herb is not outstandingly high considering that only small quantities can be consumed at one meal. Nor would it be desirable to try and eat large amounts of such a potent food. However, the vitamin and mineral content is far from being the whole story. Garlic has its own built-in secret which has taken man generations to fathom. We now know that it will prove equally effective today, as it was over 5,000 years ago, in the prevention and cure of many and varied diseases. Many things in this world change and continue to do so throughout the years, but herbs like garlic stay as they were before the birth of Christ—they are ours for the seeking—remedies which have proved effective and reliable as long as man has walked the earth.

## Secret of Garlic

What is it that makes this herb so good for us? The vitamins and protein cannot be the answer. Its power in fact is closely connected with the pungent smell, which plays a vital role in germ killing. Although this odiferous principle is only a small part of the garlic, about 2 per cent in fact, it is its life force. Scientists consider that a component of the 2 per cent called *allyl disulphate* is responsible for making garlic such a germ killer and so good for us. So it is essential to take this natural oil, there is no way of extracting the smell and leaving a perfectly good odour-free herb. To obtain the benefits from garlic you must be prepared to suffer the odour unless you obtain capsules or pearles.

## Garlic or Penicillin

It has been established that oil of garlic is about one tenth the strength of penicillin. But it must be borne in mind that with this herb we are dealing with a natural remedy that can be taken as a food or applied externally. with no ill effects. It is for this very reason that garlic is· again becoming more popular. The chemical industries are continually producing more drugs, but often the dangers lie ahead. Since the discovery of antibiotics doctors tend to prescribe them *ad lib*. One may well say, why take garlic when penicillin is ten times as strong? Well, one cannot hurry nature: it is far better to have treatment that may be slower but sure and does not cause damage to any part of the body. Drugs have saved thousands of lives and play a role in medicine and surgery. The dangers are that we can become too dependent on taking a drug and ignore the fact that often there is some nature cure which will serve the purpose and leave you in a better state of health, even if recovery takes a little longer.

## Odour-free Medicine

Nowadays we are more fortunate than those garlic lovers of old. The Herbalist with the aid of science has produced all manner of garlic medicines in capsule form (as explained in Chapter Three). So now it is possible to take even large amounts of this herb, to overcome quite serious infection, with no odour or after-effects.

# CHAPTER SEVEN

# HERBAL MEDICINE

HERBS FOR TREATMENT, or the prevention of illness and disease, have been used since man suffered sickness, which is from the time he inherited the earth. The study and practice of Herbal Medicine has been world wide. Our forefathers for centuries existed in the state of nature. They had to hunt for food and get a living from the land by the cultivation of their own crops and vegetables. For healing the sick and everyday medical treatment there was no alternative but to seek remedies from growing things. Not only were specially cultivated herbs used but remedies were sought from seeds, roots, leaves, berries and even the bark from trees. A method of trial and error was practised and man soon began to realize what was good for various complaints. All these health-giving natural remedies were handed down from father to son long before the art of writing. Gradually, as man became literate and mastered the arts of reading and writing, a complete record was built up of all plants, vegetables, herbs and other growing things, showing what illness each and every one would combat and methods of treatment. In practically every garden of the rich and poor alike a herb patch was cultivated and pots full of goodness simmered over cottagers' fires.

## Celery

An example of the manner in which many parts of certain plants can be used to enable man to live a fitter, more healthy life, free from illness, is shown by the examination of a simple plant of celery. The leaves, stalks and seeds of celery are used in herbal treatment: everything except the roots. These various parts of the celery plant contain vitamins, minerals and sulphur. Also it is a rich source of sodium. All this goodness helps to cleanse the blood and prevent rheumatism, and celery tea is wonderful for the nerves.

### The Walnut Tree

Compare our little plant of celery with a lofty 60-foot high walnut tree. From the roots to the tip of every branch a source of herbal remedies can be obtained.

### Bast

A combination of inner bark, twigs and roots used against irritants or blisters.

### Bark

Whether fresh or dried, may be effectively employed to destroy worms.

### Rusks, Bark and Leaves

Make an ideal powdered laxative.

### Leaves

After being dried and powdered, may be infused with water. Being rich in iodine they are wonderful for all thyroid complaints.

### World Wide Herbal Medicine

A remarkable thing is that the science of Herbal Medicine was being probed and practised in all parts of the world simultaneously. This was revealed when man conquered the seas and discovered other lands. In many cases identical herbs were being used for similar treatments in lands thousands of miles apart. So herbalists everywhere unbeknown to each other were in many instances using identical herbs for curing the same illness and diseases.

## Herbal Medicine in Holland

By the 16th century Herbalists all over the world were well established. During this period a Dutch Herbalist named Rembert Dodoens wrote a Dutch Herbal called *Krydeboeck*, dealing with all aspects of Herbal Medicine. This is what he had to say about garlic:

It can be used against all poisons.

Will cure coughs and toothache.

Used to strengthen loose teeth. Cures all skin diseases.

## Garlic and The Herbalist

The most renowned herbal practitioner of all time was undoubtedly Culpeper. He is considered to have been the father of herbal medicine. This is what he had to say about Garlic. "Mars owns this herb. It is a remedy for all diseases and hurts (except those which itself breeds). It provokes urine and women courses, helps the biting of mad dogs and other venomous creatures. Kills the worms in children. Cuts and voids tough phlegm, purges the head, helps the lethargy. Is a good preservative against and remedy for, any plague, sore or foul ulcer, takes away spots and blemishes in the skin, eases pains in the ears. Ripens and breaks impostunes or other swellings: and for all diseases the onions are as effectual. Its heat is vehement and all vehement things send up vapours to the brain."

It should be emphasized that the garlic pearles or capsules obtainable from Health Food Stores will not produce the effect described in the last sentence.

## Garlic and Onions

Much of the old time reputation of garlic without doubt came from its pungent smell and strength, as shown by beliefs in Folklore. Anything so pungent and strong was considered to have great power. In the quotation of that old-time herbalist Culpeper, he says, "and for all diseases onions are as effectual". Although in many ways similar to all species of onions and almost a brother of the shallot, Garlic, as already mentioned, contains *allyl disulphate*. Despite this substance being so minute, it is in fact the life force of the herb—here lies its secret.

Pioneers of the past such as Culpeper were not aware of this characteristic of garlic, it has taken the scientist years to unravel it.

### Doctors

Not only herbalists, but leading doctors ever since the first medical man or even witch doctor came into being, have believed strongly in garlic. Years ago they were compelled to rely on herbs and had no alternatives, but even in the modern age of drugs faithful followers still use garlic and other herbal remedies. A Dr. Bowles, noted English physician of long ago, made use of garlic with great success in treating patients suffering from asthma. His medicine consisted of a mixture of boiled cloves of garlic with vinegar and sugar stored in an earthenware jar. A dose consisted of a clove or two with some of the syrup.

Many medical men today, however, owing to more potent and less smelly treatments feel garlic is no longer required. They have become conditioned to antibiotics and drugs. One of the big questions is, do modern drugs destroy only harmful bacteria, leaving beneficial organisms to aid the body? Because garlic does just this, being a natural remedy that can bring nothing but beneficial results. Many illnesses have taken years, if not almost a lifetime to build up and poison the system: there is no proof that the quickest cures are best or safest. Slow but sure is sometimes the best in the long run.

## Garlic's Medicinal Power

Garlic has strong antiseptic, germicidal and disease-preventive qualities, owing partly to its high content of sulphur. Ages ago it was used as a cure for leprosy and accepted for centuries as one of the finest healing and preventive herbs ever discovered. Authors have endorsed this fact since writing came into being. They are not alone in the praise of this herb. It has been demonstrated throughout the ages. Leaders of past great empires and other famous learned men, even before the birth of The Saviour, have, after experience, supported the faith which the old time herbalist had in this stinkweed.

## Proof

Scientists of more recent years have dispelled any lingering doubts by indisputable evidence from the laboratory. This has given encouragement to those who knew from the practice of herbal medicine and natural healing that garlic, like so many herbs, would produce remarkable results if given a fair trial.

## Latest Development into Research

It is of interest to note that whilst this booklet was being prepared, experiments into the miraculous healing powers of garlic and onions continues. Once again, even in the 20th century, these time-proved ancient remedies show that drugs are far from being the only answer to the prevention of, or cure of serious illnesses.

## England Leads the Way

A casual comment by a patient that in France horses suffering from blood clots in the legs are fed on onions and garlic, led to investigations into this type of treatment by doctors of The University Department of Medicine, Newcastle upon Tyne.

*Study Group*

Twenty-two voluntary patients whose ages ranged from 19-78 years were selected for these tests. All were put on diets containing onions. The findings of these various experiments have clearly shown that some wonderful health-giving healing substance is contained in those members of the Lily family, onions, garlic and shallots. This vital ingredient causes deadly blood clots in human beings to be dispersed.

The amazing manner in which onions help cure such serious conditions is still not clear. However, these studies continue and the findings to date offer more than a ray of hope for sufferers from heart attacks, one of the major killers in Western Civilization today.

*Future*

· It is hoped that the findings of these doctors may eventually lead to natural treatment for those suffering from heart conditions. It has been shown that drugs have side effects.

# CHAPTER EIGHT

# THE AGE OF DRUGS

IT IS APPRECIATED that thousands of people today would not be alive except for drugs playing a vital role in medicine. However, there are dangerous trends and a tendency to employ the use of drugs or tranquillizers (as they are sometimes called) for almost every complaint, whether physical or mental. This fact is illustrated by the amazing evidence supplied by doctors themselves that in 1969 an estimated 11,000,000 persons in England were taking some form of drugs as sleeping pills. These unfortunate people, it seems, have lost the natural art of falling asleep, which should come automatically to humans and animals alike in a fit state of health. There are many natural remedies which would replace sleeping tablets in the field of herbal medicine, but unfortunately medical science is conditioned to prescribing drugs.

## Role of Garlic before the Advent of Drugs

During the 18th and 19th centuries garlic was extensively used by doctors. There were little or no pills of any kind. Herbal medicine has no side effects and patients do not become addicts—treatment as God provided it straight from the earth. The doctor of old really had no other choice: there was no other alternative but to follow the path of natural healing.

All herbs could be made part of the diet and used in a preventive manner, building up resistance to disease and better health for life.

The old-fashioned name of family doctor is gradually dying out under the National Health Scheme, where nearly all doctors have become civil servants. The old time doctor knew the members of all his families very well. Drugs were not used so frequently and herbs such as garlic was high on the list of medicines. In *The Home Book of Health*, written in 1878 by Dr. Gunn, M.D., references are made to the use of this herb for numerous purposes, including the cure of consumption and all diseases of the lungs: also for dropsy, fever, worms and all manner of other treatment. Dr. Gunn was one of the old family physicians unfortunately no longer with us today.

### Growth of Chemical Industries

Gradually during the last 50 years, more especially since World War II, we have changed over from natural healing herbal remedies to drugs. In this respect we have followed the Americans. This does not just apply to the use of drugs in hospitals for surgery or issued on prescription by doctors but to the entire chemical industry. We have come to accept the drug as part of our way of life and to reject natural healing methods as being old fashioned.

### The Miracle of Drugs

Scientists have made some wonderful discoveries and more and better drugs are being produced all the time. Great benefits have resulted, persons who would be in great pain with incurable diseases are helped. Soldiers on the battlefield or unfortunate victims of road accidents are given drugs to deaden the pain. Lives are being saved everywhere.

### Pain Killers

Although these drugs may only be a mild sedative, they simply remove the pain and the sufferer feels better. Pain is a natural way of sending out danger signals that all is not quite in order, so by simply removing the pain we believe we are cured. In actual fact, whatever caused the pain may still be present. In natural healing, providing the pain is bearable, when it no longer exists we know a cure has been effected. Today chemists sell a pill, tablet or powder for almost every complaint. Many people nowadays have come to accept the fact that the chemist and scientist can do everything for us. A pill to send us to sleep, one to cure a headache (probably caused by the sleeping pill), another to make the bowels function, and so on.

## Doctors' Prescriptions

For all manner of complaints where the patient is in pain the doctor will invariably issue two prescriptions. One for treatment and the other to reduce the pain. So the body has two tasks, to repair damage to the injury and at the same time overcome the effects of the drug introduced to kill the pain.

## Tranquillizers

Little soothing drugs—pep pills to make us function better. Pick-me-ups in the form of drugs for the tired, overworked housewife or harassed business man. In addition to the 11,000,000 persons who have to take sedatives in order to sleep, we now find such news items as this comment in the popular Press of 4th July, 1969— "The Government is to clamp down on prescribing of amphetamine pep pills because thousands of housewives and teenagers are hooked on them". What a tragic and unfortunate situation, for in many of these cases a change in the diet for these persons may well have worked wonders. More wholesome food, a few spoonfuls of honey and some pure brewer's yeast daily, would in many cases have brought vitality and energy to these people, some of whom may now be faced with the prospect of swallowing pep pills for life.

You may say, this is just an isolated case, so why worry? It certainly is not isolated, and a grave problem confronts us. On the 30th April, 1969, the *Daily Sketch* reports, "Britons who are hooked on aspirin". It then went on to tell us: 'More people in Britain are "hooked" on aspirin than any other drug, a chemist warned yesterday. And their addiction could be highly dangerous. Mr. J. Kerr, Senior official of the Pharmaceutical Society, told Royal Society of Health Delegates at Eastbourne, Sussex: "Aspirin is increasingly suspect of harmful effects, far beyond intestinal bleeding, which it is known to cause".'

Naturally many doctors and chemists are very concerned about these problems, and, like Mr. Kerr, serve Society well by bringing to public notice the devastating effect of drugs.

*Example of Side Effects from Drugs*

Recently an acquaintance of mine received treatment for Hypertension and made a good recovery. However, he was still taking 15 tablets a day and his problem now was to overcome the effects of these drugs. We met at the swimming baths, where he swam for about 20 minutes, a picture of health and strength: obviously his blood pressure had been brought back to near normal—the doctor had done a good job here. But what is the cost to his general state of health, for he feels the effects of the drugs very much and the object of going swimming was to try and overcome this. I wonder if garlic treatment would have cured him without leaving side effects? (See Chapter Nine—Hypertension.)

*Drug Taking on the Increase*

It is tragic that drug administration does not stay with our doctors. Pills accepted for so long find their way into our social lives in the form of pep pills and other little

4

pick-me-ups. Addicts then take to soft drugs and, what is worse, in far too many cases victims caught up in this net become addicted to hard drugs—killers.

It is hoped the fact that drugs have gained such a foothold and influence so many lives to such a great extent, may pave the way for a new era in Herbal Medicine and natural remedies.

# CHAPTER NINE

# ILLNESSES WHICH GARLIC WILL CURE

IT IS REPORTED that a Sir John Harington, writing in *The Englishman's Doctor*, in the year 1609, had this to say about garlic:—

"Garlic then have power to save from death.
Bear with it though it maketh unsavory breath,
and scorn not garlic like some that think, it
only maketh men wink and drink and stink."

It must be assumed that Sir John derived some of his muse from the words of Robert of Normandy (already quoted).

*Every Plant a Miracle*

Man, with all his power in getting to the moon and in the exploration of outer space, may never solve the mystery of life. He cannot make the simplest plant, only a crude imitation. Each and every growing thing is a remarkable laboratory of activity. Through microscopic openings in the tiniest of roots numerous minerals are chosen and by a process of combining with carbon, nitrogen and oxygen, living cells are constructed. For years vegetable juices have been considered essential for health. When the truth is known it may well be revealed that garlic is the most miraculous vegetable of all. Even allowing for exaggeration and not taking the sayings of old-time herbalists too seriously, garlic has, to say the least, a massive casebook of illnesses, ranging from the common cold to serious epidemics, which given a fair trial it will cure.

## Respiratory Infections from Colds to Bronchitis

If you have never used garlic to cure your cold or chest complaint, then let it do so for you this winter. You will be surprised at the ease and success. A lady medical practitioner, K. Nolfi, M.D., explains this in her book, *My Experiences With Living Food*. Her investigations proved that a cut clove of garlic, held on either side of the mouth between the cheeks and teeth will quickly cure a cold. She also proved the same treatment equally effective for getting loose teeth to root again and for all upper respiratory infections, including badly inflamed tonsils and glands, laryngitis, pharyngitis, bronchitis and many other illnesses. The more serious the complaint the longer the treatment and the cloves must be renewed every few hours. A cold dealt with immediately symptoms appear was cured within hours. Cloves are not held in the mouth at night. However, cut cloves of garlic rubbed on the soles of the feet will often cure a cold whilst you are asleep.

A combination of garlic in pearles with sea kelp makes ideal treatment for bronchitis, catarrh, hay fever and all chest complaints. (The pearles are odourless.)

## The Supreme Antiseptic

Many complaints are caused because of poisons building up in the system, the blood stream being unable to eliminate these impurities and toxins, which eventually may well prevent the efficient working of vital organs. Garlic should not only be used when one becomes ill, for in vegetable, tablet or capsule form it can work miracles in keeping the system free from poisons. Best used as a preventive treatment supplementary to the diet.

This antiseptic herb was used in most hospitals before the discovery of synthetic sterilizing agents. In more recent years doctors are again seeking garlic to carry out this vital function. Although not so potent as other agents, it has the advantage of not having the side effects which many synthetic ones possess.

### Skin Complaints

Dr. Nolfi also established that pimples would soon vanish if rubbed a few times with garlic. However, until the blood was put in order they would appear again. The herb is considered the most efficient cleanser of blood and tissues but must, of course, be taken internally for this purpose.

### Stomach and Intestinal Disorders

Garlic makes an ideal food and medicine for the entire digestive tract. A Dr. Weiss of Chicago reported excellent results in curing patients of diarrhoea with this herb. It was also noted that dangerous bacteria decreased, whereas healthy flora, which assists the digestive processes and vitamin production multiplied. It should be mentioned, however, that garlic taken in pearles or capsules has no laxative effect.

### Fevers

The herb is effective against fevers, particularly those of the intermittent type.

### Rheumatism

Pains of this troublesome complaint so widespread in our damp climate may well be relieved by rubbing the infected parts with cloves of cut garlic. It can also help this complaint if taken internally as it is rapidly assimilated into the blood stream and quickly taken to every part of the body.

Garlic is shown to be poison resistant, and diuretic and a wonderful prevention against all epidemic diseases.

*More serious Illness and Killer Diseases*

*The Plague*

Details have already been given of how garlic has proved a godsend in the most terrible epidemics of the Plague not only in England but throughout Europe.

*Cholera and Typhus*

The late Dr. Albert Schweitzer is said to have used garlic to cure these two dreaded illnesses.

*Asthma*

This herb has been very effective throughout history for the treatment of asthma.

*Tuberculosis*

Over 50 years ago when this disease was prevalent in many countries it was shown that garlic would work near miracles in curing victims.

*Dropsies*

An illness caused by water being held in various parts of the body, which if neglected can become very serious. Garlic can effectively overcome this complaint.

*Cancer*

Lip cancer was cured in over 93 per cent of the cases treated. In many cases only one application was necessary. (*Problems of Oncology*—March 1958.)

*Hypertension*

Various medical sources in France and Germany have for many years confirmed the belief that garlic can be used to reduce high blood pressure. In some 40 per cent of cases the blood pressure was lowered after the patients had been given garlic. This evidence was recorded by a Dr. Piotrowsky,

University of Geneva, when he wrote an article in *Praxis* in July 1948. He found the herb opened up blood vessels, thus reducing pressure and it stopped angina pains and dizziness.

## Typhoid

As far back as 1935 two Japanese doctors reported that garlic would kill off typhoid bacillus.

## Anticoagulant

One final use that has been recently found for this magic bulb is the recent discovery that it would appear to be an effective anticoagulant. Tests are being carried out at a hospital in the North of England by the addition of onions and garlic to the diets of groups of patients. Experiments are now taking place in an effort to isolate the active principle which, if successful, should greatly assist medical progress.

## Prevention

In such a little book it has only been possible to give some of the powers of this herb, sufficient it is hoped to whet your appetite and give it a try. Perhaps the greatest asset of garlic is that it keeps the body in such a fit state that serious illness is less likely. Should disease come, the garlic eater's bodily stamina is such that the effects are often quickly thrown off. The herb kills off dangerous bacteria and promotes bodily health, fitness and endurance.

It has been said that writers and others only say good things about herbs and refrain from mentioning any limitations. So we propose to examine any problems which may be caused by taking this one in particular. The fact that garlic is a very strong potent herb supports the belief of those who favour the use of, and advocate drugs for, every kind of treatment. There is, however, an important difference. Garlic does not have 'side-effects', but the same thing cannot be said about drugs and if the wrong one is administered by mistake or the dosage is excessive, results can be dangerous. The answer in many cases is for the individual to try the herb.

Although persons enjoying good health and not suffering from digestive disorders should be able to eat garlic and onions alike, it is an accepted fact that some people are unable to, or dislike eating raw onions, so garlic would be too strong for them. Just as some people cannot take certain drugs, so others may be allergic to garlic. Moderation, or use of 'pearles' is the answer. Large doses of anything, whether it be food or medicine, present dangers, and your 'pearle' should contain the correct dosage of good quality oil, not just the largest amount. But the fact remains that garlic improves the digestive system, as has been shown.

## Objections to Garlic

'It has a vehement heat and hot things send up vapours to the brain.' These are not the words of a person against the use of this herb, but have been quoted by eminent men and herbalists for centuries. So for Cholera it is not suitable treatment, 'It will add fuel to the fire'. To quote some more ancient advice, 'Let it be taken inwardly with moderation: outwardly you may be more bold with it'.

One of the problems with garlic, and more particularly onions, in the kitchen is that peeling them makes people cry! The answer is not to lean over the chopping board but to stand reasonably upright, or sit with arms extended. (Washing the hands in a little salt water afterwards removes most of the smell.) This will not necessarily completely eliminate the problem and it is surprising that onion should present more difficulty than the stronger garlic in this respect, and readers who do not wish to burst into tears at the sight of an onion may wish to know that little onion capsules containing the natural flavour essence can be bought at some Health Food Stores. These are simply dropped in the stew or hot-pot or whatever you are cooking. Garlic flavour essence capsules or "Buds" are also sold, but note that while these are useful for culinary purposes they do not necessarily retain all the essential oil as do Pearles.

In olden times it was considered that garlic should not be taken by bad tempered persons because it was too hot for them. It was considered that the strength of the herb made it better suited to persons of more stable dispositions and even temper, with milder and more gentle natures!

No one in their right senses would wish to consume large amounts of garlic for breakfast, dinner and tea. 'Enough is as good as a feast'. On the other hand, it must be stressed that the great germ-destroying and health-giving properties of this herb make it desirable as a normal and regular addition to the diet. I have yet to find anyone who became ill through eating garlic. We cannot say this about drugs. On the contrary, almost every daily newspaper contains some tragic account of persons from all walks of life taking an overdose of drugs by accident or design, and thereby damaging their health and, in some cases, losing their lives.

# CHAPTER TEN

# INTRODUCING GARLIC INTO THE KITCHEN

MANY NATIONS MAKE the skill of cookery equal, if not superior to all the other arts. The Chinese place food preparation high on their list of artistic achievements—believing, and rightly so, that a man becomes what he eats. The French share the Chinese view and have for long been masters at preparing appetizing dishes. The foods of these two nations have become world famous and can be obtained practically anywhere. Garlic, like such exquisite preparations as soya sauce, will completely dominate a meal if used to excess. The right amount will bring out all the flavours, making the dish the more appetizing, delicious, and above all, really health-giving. With a repast that has been garnished with this herb the actual taste of garlic should not be so noticeably present. It should influence the meal in such a subtle way and to such an extent that if it is omitted all would immediately be aware that something is lacking.

## Not too much but enough

Recipes are often given in cookery books concerning garlic, when it is suggested that a cut clove be rubbed around the salad bowl or saucepan. Well, this is all very fine as an introduction. If you really want to get to know this herb and obtain full benefits from it your ration must be increased, even if gradually.

## Garlic Salt

This makes a fine substitute for sea or biochemic salt. Sold by most Health Food shops, it is a pure food prepared simply from dehydrated cloves of garlic. Such a preparation is an ideal way of getting small quantities of this herb at a moment's notice. This can be adapted in a similar way to that by which people in the East take soya sauce with meals.

## Improves Digestion

People opposed to the use of garlic in cooking often assume that it is indigestible. On the contrary, it greatly aids the digestive processes and promotes the health of the stomach. A valuable food that makes for physical strength and well-being.

## Culinary Uses

There are endless ways of using garlic. This herb is so versatile that a book could be written on using it in the kitchen, for any savoury cooking is enhanced by it. *Simple ways of preparation.* After the skin has been removed from the cloves they can be thinly sliced and fried in butter or nut oil till golden brown and used as flavouring. The cloves may be chopped very fine and used in dishes. Juice can be obtained from cloves (there is a special garlic squeezer for this). The salad bowl, fish, meat, or pan may be rubbed with garlic before commencing the cooking.

To be moderate in all things, this is the best way to health and happiness. This applies to eating, more especially with such a strong, vital, health-giving herb as garlic. There are some preparations very rich in garlic, in fact, simply oozing with it. These certainly are not advocated for people in Western society and in only limited amounts for those in hot or tropical countries.

## Soups

A clove of garlic chopped very fine and added to a pan of soup will completely transform it. Try it and see for yourself

—you will enjoy a much more tasty bowl of soup and have the health-giving benefits of this herb.

### Salads

Cut a clove of garlic and rub it all round the salad bowl and a fine flavour will result. An ideal way of introducing a stranger to garlic. Another method is to cut up some small squares of bread and allow a few drops of olive oil to soak into them. After rubbing the pieces of bread all over with cut garlic, place them in the bottom of the salad bowl. After leaving for about twenty minutes, toss the salad which is then ready to serve. This is a French way of serving salads with garlic, they call the squares of bread 'capons' which are discarded after they have enhanced the salad. It will make the bowl of salad the finest you have ever tasted.

### Meat Dishes

Having removed the skins from cloves of garlic, make a number of incisions in the joint of pork, lamb or mutton, and insert cloves of garlic (3 to 6 according to the weight of the meat). This treatment will make the joint much more tender and bring out the best flavours.

### Roasted Garlic

Prepare cloves of garlic and place with a little nut or vegetable oil in a tin or dish: roast till slightly golden. This will add that little extra to any meal.

During the preparation of salads on the continent, blanched endive leaves and cultivated dandelion are often used as well as lettuce.

### Garlic Loaf

*Ingredients:* 1 large clove garlic; 1 large loaf of the lighter kind, such as Nimble or milk loaf; enough butter to spread on both sides of every slice.

Cut the entire loaf, being careful not to completely sever the slices. Crush the clove of garlic and incorporate it into the butter and leave it for some 20 mins. Spread the butter on both sides of the slices of bread. After pressing the loaf together heat in oven till crisp.

### Spanish Dish. Bean and Garlic Soup

*Ingredients:* 8 cloves of garlic, quarter to half a pint of dried beans (soya or haricot), amount of beans depends on size of cloves, 2 teaspoonfuls of sea salt.

Place beans in container and add 2 pints of cold water and leave overnight. Bring beans to the boil, then add garlic with the salt and simmer for about one and a half to two hours or until the beans become quite tender. On serving, butter or a tablespoonful of olive or other vegetable oil may be added. Should be sufficient for four persons.

### Garlic Butter

*Ingredients:* 4 cloves of garlic used to every quarter pound of butter.

Peel the cloves and pound them together with the butter. This is really quite a strong preparation, especially if the cloves are fairly large. Therefore, one clove may be used at first to acquire the taste and test the strength.

### Garlic Forcemeat. Farce D'Ail

May be used as cold *hors-d'oeuvre* or similar dishes.

*Ingredients:* 6 yolks of hard boiled eggs, 6 blanched cloves of garlic, an amount of fresh butter equal to about half the total amount of eggs and garlic.

The yolks and garlic are pounded in a mortar. The butter is then added, blended with the yolks and garlic and passed through a sieve.

### Garlic Toast

A very popular dish in the S.W. of France known as

*Rotie à L'ail.* A number of pieces of wholemeal bread are lightly toasted. The toast is then spread with garlic *purée*, sprinkled with grated breadcrumbs and olive or nut oil. It is then left in oven till brown.

## Garlic Purée

A number of cloves of garlic are blanched, then cooked in butter or vegetable oil. Then add one dessertspoonful of thick sauce for each clove of garlic—blend and sieve. This *purée* is served as an accompanying dish with other meals.

## Bechamel Sauce

An ideal sauce for preparing the garlic *Purée*. To make 1 pint.

Stir one pint of boiling milk into a cup of white *roux* (mixture of butter and flour in equal portions). Then mix. Afterwards add 1 oz. diced lean veal, 1 teaspoonful chopped onion or shallot. Cook in butter. Add sprig of thyme, a little bay leaf and grated nutmeg. Simmer 10-15 mins. Strain through cloth.

## Garlic Oil

Blanch 10 cloves garlic. After draining, pound in mortar till fine paste is formed. Add 1 cup olive oil. Then pass through muslin cloth. This makes a fine oil for seasoning salads.

## Sausage Casserole with Cider

*Ingredients:* 6-8 sausages, 1 cup cider, 3 cloves garlic, 3 shallots, 2 or 3 apples, sage, parsley, sea salt, pepper.

After rolling sausages in flour they are fried lightly, using vegetable or nut oil. Core apples and slice them up. Chop up shallots. Put sliced apples and shallots in layers in casserole dish with the sausages. Add finely chopped sage, garlic and parsley. Season with salt and pepper, add the cider. Cover and cook for one hour in medium oven. Serves 3 to 4 persons.

## Stuffed Steak Rolls

*Ingredients:* 1 to 2 lb. of steak, 1 cup red wine, stuffing, breadcrumbs, 3 rashers bacon, 2 cloves finely chopped garlic, 1 dessertspoonful each of chopped onion, celery and parsley.

Cut steak and bacon into strips. Combine the stuffing and spread onto the strips. Roll up and secure with wooden toothpicks. Roll lightly in flour and brown in a little shortening. Add liquid and simmer in a medium oven for two hours.

## Garlic Capons

Or *Chapons A L'ail* as they are called in S.W. France. These simply consist of crusts of bread which are rubbed with raw garlic and seasoned with oil, salt, vinegar and pepper. These are added to all manner of green salads, in particular to curly chicory.

## Chopped or Grated Garlic

This in French cooking is called *Ail Haché Rapé*. In fact the French do not actually chop this herb: they insist that it is either pounded or grated up. It then may be added to any amount of dishes. Best results are obtained if the garlic is only added to the remainder of the ingredients at the last moment. Care should be taken not to fry the garlic much because this will make the meal far too pungent.

When a point of garlic is referred to in French cooking it means the smallest amount that can be gathered on the point of a knife.

## Garlic Pickle

*Ingredients:* 2 cloves of garlic, 2 quarts white vinegar, 4 oz. mustard seed, 2 oz. ginger, 2 oz. chillies, 2 oz. turmeric, 6 oz. sea salt.

Measure 1 pint of water and bring to boil after adding the salt. At boiling point pour it over the ginger. Then let it stand for about one week. After peeling garlic, sprinkle with salt and leave for 48 hours. Finally put garlic, mustard seed, ginger, chillies and turmeric in jar, pouring on the vinegar. After sealing off, the contents must stand for 2-3 days before being ready for use.

## Garlic Vinegar

*Ingredients:* 1 pint vinegar, 8-10 cloves garlic, small amount sea salt.

Peel and crush cloves of garlic. When the vinegar has been brought to the boil, pour over the crushed cloves similar to the manner of brewing tea. Allow to cool, then pour into a jar and cover. After 15-20 days strain and your vinegar is ready for use.

## Make Garlic Part of Your Diet

If you have never had garlic before, do make an attempt to try this fine food. It is said that variety is the spice of life, and as far as cooking goes this herb will bring infinite variety. The art, which will be quickly acquired, is to use not too much nor too little but just the right amount. There is practically no limit to its addition in one form or another to every savoury meal—juiced or grated as finely as possible and at first used very sparingly till fondness has been stimulated. The art of serving any meal with garlic is to use it modestly, incorporating it into all the other flavours.

## Problem of the Odour

The persistent odour of garlic is unfortunate. Ways of counteracting this include: chewing a fresh sprig of parsley, eating beetroot, or drinking milk after a meal served with garlic. Parsley, the most effective deodorant, rich in vitamin C, is a good addition to the diet of everyone. A daily intake of this vitamin is essential for good health.